What the Children's Blizzard of 1888?

by Steve Korté

illustrated by Dede Putra

Penguin Workshop

For Juliette—SK

PENGUIN WORKSHOP
An imprint of Penguin Random House LLC, New York

First published in the United States of America by Penguin Workshop,
an imprint of Penguin Random House LLC, New York, 2023

Visit us online at penguinrandomhouse.com.

Library of Congress Cataloging-in-Publication Data is available.

Printed in the United States of America

ISBN 9780593520710 (paperback)   10 9 8 7 6 5 4 3 2 1 WOR
ISBN 9780593520727 (library binding)   10 9 8 7 6 5 4 3 2 1 WOR

Contents

What Was the Children's Blizzard of 1888?

January 12, 1888, started out as an unusually warm and sunny winter day in much of the central and midwestern parts of the United States. This area was known as the Great Plains.

1

In the days leading up to January 12, the temperature in that region had rarely gotten above zero degrees. That was not a surprise to the people who lived there. Winters in the Great Plains were almost always brutally cold.

But the weather surprised everyone on January 12, as unusually warm temperatures hit the region. In the town of Aberdeen, in what is now South Dakota, the temperature rose to twenty-eight degrees. That might not seem very warm, but compared to a temperature of zero, it felt wonderful. Throughout the Great Plains, children walked to schools without gloves or hats. Many of the children wore just a light jacket. Farmers went outside to do their chores without their overcoats. The clear, sunny skies and warmer temperature were a welcome relief. In addition, there were no warnings about cold weather returning to the area any time soon.

But that afternoon, the weather suddenly changed. The sunny skies disappeared. Children and teachers looked out the windows of their schoolrooms and watched nervously as a cloud of darkness swept across the skies.

Temperatures suddenly plunged to forty-seven degrees below zero in some areas. Winds started howling, gusting at more than seventy miles an hour. A mixture of ice and snow started falling.

The violent storm hit without warning. Farmers out in the fields tried to find their way back home, but the snow was so thick and the winds so strong that they couldn't see. The snow started blowing sideways, freezing the eyelids of anyone standing outside. Children were trapped in their classrooms as the storm battered their schoolhouses. Some students made the difficult decision to brave the roaring winds and blinding snow as they attempted to return to their homes.

A day that had started so happily soon acquired a new and terrible name. The horrible storm on January 12 would soon be known as the Children's Blizzard of 1888.

CHAPTER 1
New Arrivals

During the 1800s, the population of the United States grew quickly. Many new immigrants arrived from Europe. During the years between 1850 and 1890, the population of the United States grew from twenty-three million to sixty-three million, almost tripling the number of people living there. Most of these immigrants were very poor, arriving without jobs or money. Many found homes in crowded and usually run-down apartment buildings in New York City, Boston, Philadelphia, and other big cities. But tens of thousands of other immigrants decided to make a second journey after they arrived in the United States. They traveled west.

In 1888, there were only thirty-eight states in America. The large midwestern region of the country that now includes the states of Montana, North and South Dakota, Idaho, and Wyoming was divided into what were known as federal territories. They were part of an even larger area known as the Great Plains, which included the entire states of Kansas and Nebraska, along with parts of Colorado, Iowa, Minnesota, Missouri, Montana, New Mexico, Oklahoma, Texas, and southern portions of Canada.

1888

8

The midwestern section of the Great Plains was sometimes also called the prairie. It was mostly flat and ready for farming. Land stretched as far as you could see in every direction. Unlike the crowded cities on the East Coast, the prairie offered space. And it also offered an opportunity for many to start a new life.

The immigrants who traveled west came from many countries, including Germany, Russia, Sweden, and Norway. Some journeyed to America so that they could worship as they pleased. Others were hoping to escape poverty. The one thing that almost all of them had in common was that they wanted to start a new life.

Abraham Lincoln

In 1862, President Abraham Lincoln signed into law the Homestead Act. This new law allowed any US citizen to buy land in the Great Plains for a low price. A flood of people took advantage of the offer and purchased farmlands.

Prior to the Homestead Act, the Great Plains had been the home of many large Indian nations, including the Cheyenne, the Sioux, the Comanche, and the Kiowa. Native Americans had been living on this land for thousands of years, and they farmed and hunted buffalo across the flat, grassy plains. There were millions of large, shaggy buffalo to be found on the Great Plains, and Native Americans found uses for almost every part of the buffalo they killed—eating the meat, making blankets from the fur, and using their dried bones as tools.

Before the white settlers started arriving in the Great Plains, the US government forced most of the Native Americans to move to reservations, which were government-owned lands established just for them. Land on the reservations was usually not as good for farming, and there were far fewer buffalo to be found. Life on the reservations was very difficult for most of the people who were forced to live there.

The Homestead Act

The Homestead Act of 1862 guaranteed that any person—US or foreign born—who was a US citizen or filing the paperwork to become one could purchase land in the Great Plains. For a payment of only eighteen dollars (about five hundred dollars today), a person would receive 160 acres of land, which they had to promise to live on and farm for five years. By the end of 1865, over a million acres of land had been distributed via the Homestead Act.

After the Civil War, the 1866 Civil Rights Act and the Fourteenth Amendment guaranteed that Southern African Americans were eligible to purchase land as well.

After the Native Americans were forced out of the Great Plains, immigrants arrived by the thousands. During the 1880s, the Dakota Territory—now known as North and South Dakota—grew from a population of 135,000 people to over half a million. More than 75,000 new farms were established there.

Most of the new settlers in the Great Plains could not afford building supplies and did not have access to materials to construct sturdy houses.

There were far fewer trees on the prairie than in the woodlands, which meant that log cabins were rarely an option. Instead, many of the settlers lived in sod houses or dugouts. The sod house—also known as a soddy—was a tiny home made up of a layer of hardened soil mixed with roots. Long strips of soil and roots were chopped to make sod bricks. These were then stacked on top of each other to form the walls of the house. Roofs were made of branches, roots, and hay, topped with a layer of sod.

Sod houses had many drawbacks. They were, after all, made of only a layer of dirt and roots. Anything could be living in that soil. Snakes and small animals such as gophers sometimes emerged from the walls, dirt got into food and clothing, and sod houses also leaked when it rained. As one settler recalled, "I would wake up with dirty water running through my hair."

Sod houses were only slightly better than dugout dwellings, which were merely caves dug into the side of a hill. Sometimes only a blanket covered the open entrance to the dugout.

Different types of schoolhouses could be found in the Great Plains. The best ones were two-story wooden buildings that had room for more than one classroom. But those types of

schoolhouses were limited to the most populated
sections of the prairie. Students in more isolated
areas were not as lucky. They studied in one-room
schoolhouses, sometimes made of sod.

CHAPTER 2
Life on the Great Plains

Life for the new settlers on the wide-open and windy prairie was isolated and often lonely. Most people lived far away from their neighbors, and it was hard to communicate with others. Telephones had only recently been invented, and they were mostly available in large cities. There were very few newspapers, and the ones that were available often arrived days late. There was no radio or television yet.

1876 telephone

21

What little public transportation there was consisted of horse-drawn wagons or carriages or sleighs—no cars or buses yet—so children in the Great Plains often had to walk miles every day to get to and from their schools.

Farming the prairie land could be difficult work and was sometimes even dangerous. One of the hardships facing the farmers was fire. Long periods without rain created droughts that sometimes led to grass fires. In 1887, one family in the Dakota Territory watched helplessly as a prairie fire rapidly swept through a huge area of dry grass on their land. They reported that clouds of smoke blocked out the sun, and the heat was unbearable.

In addition to the deadly fires, the settlers were forced to deal with swarms of hungry grasshoppers. These flying insects were a now-extinct species of Rocky Mountain locust. They would arrive at the end of summer when crops were fully grown. Suddenly, the sky above the fields

Rocky Mountain locust

would turn dark as a swarm of grasshoppers descended from the sky and consumed a farmer's entire crop. According to some settlers, the swarm could be a mile high and hundreds of miles wide, with perhaps billions of bugs devouring the crops.

"They drifted over in such clouds as to blacken the whole heavens, and with such a buzzing roaring noise that it could be heard a long time before they came over us," wrote one settler about several locust invasions in the 1870s.

But worse than the fires and grasshoppers were the long and brutal winters that descended on the Great Plains every year. Winters on the prairie brought months of howling winds, snow and sleet, gigantic lightning storms, and bitter cold.

Lars Stavig

A Norwegian immigrant named Lars Stavig wrote this about winters in the Dakota Territory: "When the fierce winds swept the blinding snow over hill and valley, everything looked alike and it was almost impossible to find your way. Many a brave pioneer who came out here with great hopes and plans for a long, prosperous, and happy life, in his own home and with his family, was cut down in the prime of life. This cruel, treacherous enemy, the blizzard spared no one."

What Is a Blizzard?

A blizzard is a severe snowstorm that combines low temperatures, strong winds, and large amounts of falling snow. Not every snowstorm is a blizzard, though. To be classified as a blizzard, the winds must be greater than or equal to thirty-five miles per hour. Anything with lower wind speeds than that is just a snowstorm.

In her book *The Long Winter*, Laura Ingalls Wilder wrote about growing up in the Dakota Territory town of De Smet during the brutal winter of 1880 to 1881. Several dangerous snowstorms hit De Smet between October and April, trapping her family in their home, where they almost starved.

"There was nothing in the world but cold and dark . . . and winds blowing," Wilder wrote. "The storm was always there, outside the walls, waiting sometimes, then pouncing, shaking the house, roaring, snarling, and screaming in rage."

Residents in the Great Plains worked long, tiring hours as they farmed their new land. They faced many hardships. When a winter storm descended, often without warning, it brought more than cold weather. It also brought fear, hunger, sorrow, and sometimes loss of life. Some of the settlers who came to the region were not prepared to deal with such extreme weather, and they were driven away by the deadly winters. But many more were determined to make a fresh start on the prairie. They hoped to conquer their 160 acres and make better lives for their families. They would not let the weather defeat them.

Laura Ingalls Wilder (1867–1957)

Laura Ingalls Wilder was an American author who wrote a series of eight Little House on the Prairie books that were published between 1932 and 1943. The books were based on her childhood memories of growing up in Wisconsin, Kansas, Minnesota, and the Dakota Territory. Although she didn't graduate from high school, she became a teacher when she was only fifteen years old and taught in one-room schoolhouses.

She wrote her first book in 1930 when she was sixty-three years old and planned to call it *When Grandma Was a Little Girl*. It was published in 1932 as *Little House in the Big Woods* and was an instant success. It and the subsequent seven Little House books have been continuously in print since then and have been translated into forty languages. The books were the inspiration for a successful TV series that ran from 1974 to 1983.

CHAPTER 3
The Calm Before the Storm

The first weeks of January in 1888 were brutally cold on the Great Plains. Most days the temperatures sank below zero degrees. In the Dakota Territory town of Bismarck, the lows were usually around minus thirty. But there was a sudden change of temperature in the region on Thursday, January 12, 1888. On that morning, unseasonably warm air pushed north from the Gulf of Mexico. Temperatures in much of the Midwest rose above freezing. The dramatic change must have felt like spring weather to the residents of the Great Plains! That morning, farmers went back into their fields to work and looked after their animals. Children walked to school that morning and didn't even bother to wear their hats, gloves, wool coats, or sturdy boots. The very cold weather had kept some students at home during the previous weeks, but classrooms were full again on January 12.

What almost no one in the region knew, though, was that a major change was on its way.

The science of weather forecasting was still new in the United States. It wasn't until 1870 that Congress authorized the establishment of a national weather-reporting agency. It was to be run by the US Army Signal Corps, and its headquarters would be located in Washington, DC. In 1887, General Adolphus W. Greely, who had once explored the Arctic, was chosen to head the agency. Individual soldiers worked as weather

General Adolphus W. Greely

observers in stations around the country, and they sent out their weather reports by telegram to local authorities and newspapers. When sudden, dangerous winter weather was predicted, the Signal Corps would send out a telegram containing a "cold wave warning." Those reports would then be printed in local newspapers and hopefully spread by word of mouth.

In early 1888, the person in charge of monitoring the weather for most of the Great Plains was army lieutenant Thomas Woodruff. He was stationed in the weather forecasting office in Saint Paul, Minnesota. It was close to midnight on Wednesday, January 11, when Woodruff finalized his weather forecast for the next day. He picked up a pen, filled it with black ink, and wrote the

Lieutenant Thomas Woodruff

following forecast for the Dakota Territory: "For Saint Paul, Minneapolis and vicinity: Warmer weather with snow, fresh southerly winds becoming variable. For Dakota: Snow, warmer, followed in the western portion by colder weather, fresh to high winds generally becoming northerly."

The Technology of the Telegram

In 1816, an English scientist named Francis Ronalds invented the first working electric telegraph machine, which could be used to send electrical signals via wires to other telegraph machines. It was the fastest way for people to connect with each other over long distances.

From 1837 to 1838, the American inventor Samuel Morse worked with a few other men to develop a system that transformed the electrical signals into words. It became known as the Morse code.

A telegraph operator would press down on a device that would send out a series of long or short electrical sounds, which could then be heard on another machine. Each letter in the alphabet matched up with a series of short or long pulses—often called dots and dashes. For example, the letter *A* was one short pulse, followed by one long pulse. The person at the other end of the telegraph line would then write down each letter to form a message. That message—delivered as a printed letter—is called a telegram.

Woodruff chose not to issue a more serious cold wave warning for the region but instead merely wrote that heavy snow was coming. He handed the piece of paper containing his forecast to a soldier and instructed him to send it by telegraph to other Signal Corps weather offices, the Associated Press, major newspapers in the Great Plains, and the Saint Paul District Telegraph Company in Minnesota.

Woodruff's forecast failed to mention that a large mass of cold air from Canada was rushing south, heading toward the Midwest. When cold air meets warm, moist air, it's the perfect condition to create a storm.

By the time Signal Corps weather forecasters sent out telegrams on the morning of January 12 revising their initial forecast to warn about a blizzard heading toward the Great Plains, it was too late. Too many people were already outdoors and enjoying the warmer weather.

CHAPTER 4
The Blizzard

The deadly blizzard that hit the Great Plains in January 1888 was not the first one to hit the region. The first blizzard to be recorded by the Army Signal Corps occurred in 1873 and killed about seventy people in Minnesota. In October 1880, a series of blizzards blasted the upper Midwest for so many months that the people there called it the Snow Winter. These storms lasted so long that they prevented trains from delivering supplies because the tracks were covered with deep snow. Residents were unable to get food or coal for heating. In some areas, snow from that first October storm was still on the ground the following May.

In the winter of 1886 to 1887, a series of deadly blizzards hit the Great Plains and lasted for several months. It became known as the Winter of Blue Snow, and its storms nearly killed off the entire cattle population in the Dakota Territory. Millions of cattle died of exhaustion, suffocated when their nostrils filled with snow, or froze to death when they became trapped within snowbanks. After the storm, dozens of cattle ranches were forced to close.

And then, on January 12, 1888, another storm struck. All across the Midwest, the cold air that had formed over Canada crashed into the warm, moist air from the Gulf of Mexico. The warm air froze into snow and ice crystals. The fast-moving snowstorm quickly became a blizzard. The storm first struck Montana in the morning. It then moved through the Dakota Territory in the early afternoon and reached Nebraska around three o'clock in the afternoon. Blue skies disappeared as thick black clouds rolled in. Temperatures plunged across the region. In the northern Dakota Territory, the temperature dropped to forty below zero, with sixty-mile-per-hour winds whipping the snow.

An American schoolhouse in the 1880s

A family living on the Great Plains, 1886

General Adolphus W. Greely of the US Army Signal Corps

Nebraska settlers who received land from the Homestead Act of 1862

Two Cheyenne men, circa 1880

A family with their sod house or "soddy," circa 1880

Francis Ronalds, inventor of the first working electric telegraph machine

Samuel Morse, who helped invent a code for sending telegrams

A train car moves between two walls of snow caused by
the 1880 "Snow Winter" storm.

Children's snow clothes, 1880s

1880s schoolchildren with their teachers

Settler woman with children in the Dakota Territory, circa 1885

A train goes through the Great Plains, 1890.

New York City during its own 1888 blizzard

Outside a schoolhouse in the town of Huron in the Dakota Territory, the children were playing during recess. Oscar Coursey was one of those schoolchildren, and he remembered what happened as the storm approached.

"The air was so charged with electricity that a poker held near a hot stove would emit sparks; and one's hair would leap toward a rubber comb if held near it," he said. "At recess, during the forenoon, we were all out playing in our shirtsleeves, without hats or mittens.

Suddenly we looked up and saw something coming rolling toward us with great fury from the northwest, and making a loud noise. It hit the building with such force that it nearly moved it off its cobble-stone foundation. And the

roar of the wind was indescribable. [The] wind and the snow beating against the frame building made such a terrible noise that the teacher had to scream into each child's ear, to make it hear . . ."

The blizzard's snow was a powdery mix of frozen water that made it almost impossible to see anything in front of you. People who were trapped outside in the storm didn't know which way to go in search of safety. There were reports of people dying in their own yards, just feet away from their own homes, because they couldn't see them. Some people put lamps in their windows to help those who were outside, but these lights were rarely visible.

Most of the people who died during the blizzard were trying to reach their homes, only to lose their way in the raging snowstorm.

The storm came to be known as the "Children's Blizzard of 1888" because so many of its victims were children trying to make their way home from school that day. Some of the children were found dead not far from shelter. There were many sad stories about what happened on January 12. There were also inspiring tales of bravery.

CHAPTER 5
"Nebraska's Fearless Maid"

Many stories that were later told about the blizzard involved courageous schoolteachers who helped their students. Some of these teachers

Minnie Mae Freeman

were barely older than the children they taught. Minnie Mae Freeman was probably still a teenager when she was teaching students at the Midvale School in rural Nebraska on January 12. Her students ranged in age from about five to fifteen. As the blizzard hit her one-room sod schoolhouse, the temperature outside plunged to twenty degrees below zero.

Hail smashed into the windows, and fierce winds tore the leather hinges off the door and blew the door open. Some of the older boys repaired the hinges, but the door burst open again. The boys then nailed it shut.

"I put my cloak on and was wondering what I was going to do," Minnie later remembered. "Then I happened to think of a ball of twine I had taken away from a little fellow named Frankie Gibben, who was playing with it during school hours. I began tying the children together, and when I had completed this task I awaited developments."

Suddenly, a heavy gust of wind ripped off a corner of the tar-paper-and-sod roof of the schoolhouse, leaving a hole large enough that snow started falling into the classroom. Minnie

was worried that the building might collapse in the storm, and they would all freeze. She made the difficult decision to leave the schoolhouse and lead her students to safety.

Minnie and her students, each child tied to another one, climbed through a window and stepped into the knee-deep snow. She hoped to lead them to the closest home, which was about three quarters of a mile away from the schoolhouse.

"I've never felt such a wind," she later told a

newspaper reporter. "It blew the snow so hard that the flakes stung your face like arrows. All you could see ahead of you was a blinding, blowing sheet of snow."

She added, "I thought at one time we should be lost, and I came near losing hope, for I was nearly exhausted. You see, I was carrying the smallest child—a little girl—and my talking to the children and urging them to keep up their spirits, tired me very much."

Fortunately, Minnie and her chain of more than a dozen schoolchildren connected by Frankie Gibben's twine all found their way to shelter and survived. Minnie did not want to accept any praise for her actions, but her name and the tale of what she had done were among the first to come out of the storm. On January 18, the *Omaha Daily Bee* newspaper told of Minnie's actions under the headline "A Heroine of the Storm."

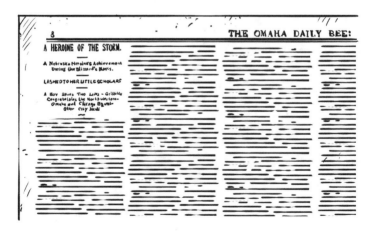

Soon, Minnie's name began to appear in local and national newspapers. Some people even began to refer to the storm as the "Minnie Freeman Blizzard." A song called "Thirteen Were Saved, or Nebraska's Fearless Maid" was written in Minnie's honor.

Due to all the publicity, Minnie received many gifts and letters from admirers. It was reported that she even received more than two hundred marriage proposals!

"Thirteen Were Saved"

Here are some of the lyrics to the song "Thirteen Were Saved," written by William Vincent to honor the young schoolteacher Minnie Freeman:

A little schoolhouse stood alone,

Upon a prairie bare;

And thirteen little children came,

One winter morning fair;

But awful storm-clouds suddenly

Obscured the sun and sky,

And terror filled each little heart,

And tears came in the eye.

Swiftly came the rushing noise,

As swiftly came the snow,

All hidden from the landscape then,

They knew not where to go;

The brave girl gathered them about,

And prayed to God for aid,

Then quick as thought from simple cord,

A band of union made.

The Blizzard of 1888 glass mural

Today, a mural depicting Minnie in the snow can be seen at the Nebraska State Capitol building. But during her lifetime, Minnie always stated that she never wanted to be called a hero.

"Too much has already been said of an act of simple duty," she wrote in a letter to the *Omaha Daily Bee*.

CHAPTER 6
Heroes in the Storm

Minnie Freeman was just one of many teachers who were forced to choose between possibly freezing in a schoolroom or sending students home in the storm. When the blizzard hit Pawnee City, Nebraska, a teacher named Seymour Dopp decided to keep his students in his one-room schoolhouse. They stayed overnight, burning wood to keep warm.

The next day, anxious parents struggled through five-foot-high snowdrifts to reach the schoolhouse and rescue their children. Dopp's decision saved the lives of his seventeen students.

In the town of O'Neill, Nebraska, a teacher named Grace McCoy also chose to keep her students in the classroom overnight. As the storm raged outside their schoolhouse, Grace worried that she and her students had no coal or wood to burn, and nothing to eat.

"Night had come on with its fury of snow and wind," she said. "We decided to burn the seats and desks. That was easier to say than to do. But the children were looking up into my face and saying: 'My feet are so cold, and my hands are cold, too.' We had a small hatchet and the boys wore heavy boots, so we were able to break up a seat or two at a time, and we left the stove door open to give us light."

In Hastings, Nebraska, a college professor named F. M. Hickock became a local hero during the storm. He was blind but able to find his way around town without help. When the blizzard hit, Professor Hickock made his way to the local elementary school. He instructed the schoolchildren to hold hands and stay connected to each other. Hickock was able to keep his

sense of direction in the blowing snow, and he miraculously led the children to safety through the storm.

Seventeen-year-old teacher Grace Kent had grown up on the prairie, and she immediately recognized the danger of the threatening clouds moving toward her Dakota Territory schoolhouse. She quickly wrapped her students in her own

spare clothing. She sent the older children home. She then escorted the younger children safely to their homes, just as the storm hit. Grace then tried to find her way to her father's home, but the storm grew stronger. She couldn't see anything around her and soon realized that she was lost. Unable to keep walking, Grace crawled into a small shed that was used for sheep. She spent the night there, huddled against the animals.

When a rescue party arrived the next morning, Grace was still alive, but her feet were frostbitten. They had to be surgically removed to save her life.

Lois Royce was a teacher in Nebraska. She spent the night of the storm out on the open prairie with three of her students—a six-year-old girl and two nine-year-old boys. She covered the children with her coat, but all three children died in her arms during the night. Both of Lois's feet suffered from severe frostbite, but somehow she survived overnight. The next morning, Lois crawled a quarter of a mile to the nearest farmhouse.

Two weeks before the storm, nineteen-year-old Etta Shattuck had quit her job as a schoolteacher

Etta Shattuck

in a rural part of Nebraska. But on January 12 she needed to visit her one-room schoolhouse so that she could collect her final paycheck. She was not far from her house when the blizzard struck. As the storm howled around her, Etta became too cold and weak to walk. She crawled into a haystack. As night fell, the hay froze around her. Etta's legs, which were sticking out of the haystack, developed frostbite. It wasn't until three days later, on Sunday, January 15, that a farmer

68

discovered Etta in the haystack. Miraculously, she was still alive. Unfortunately, doctors were forced to remove both of her legs below the knees.

The heroic actions of so many teachers in the Great Plains led to the creation of the Heroine Fund. Several newspapers set up campaigns to raise money and help teachers who were facing medical expenses after the blizzard. By the end of February, the fund had raised over $11,000 (more than $343,000 today).

The fund sent $3,752 to the family of Etta Shattuck, who had died early on the morning of February 6. She was one of many victims of the storm who would die in the months after the blizzard of injuries they had suffered during it.

69

Frostbite and Hypothermia

Frostbite and hypothermia are two dangerous conditions caused by exposure to cold.

Frostbite occurs when living tissues (such as skin) freeze, and it usually affects hands and feet. It is the body's way of protecting important organs, such as the heart, lungs, and brain. When a person is exposed to cold temperatures, the blood retreats to those vital organs, leaving remote body parts such as fingers and toes more vulnerable. During a blizzard, it can take only a few minutes for exposed fingers to become frostbitten, especially if they are wet.

Hypothermia occurs when a person's body temperature drops below ninety-five degrees. A person with hypothermia will start shivering, which is the body's way of trying to stay warm. They may become confused and grow very weary.

Once the shivering stops, the body starts to shut down.

The best remedy for hypothermia is to wrap a person in warm blankets and take them to the hospital. The cure for frostbite is to soak the affected body parts in warm water for at least thirty minutes, until the skin color becomes normal and feeling returns. Don't try to massage the area. Back in the 1800s, it was wrongly believed that the best remedy for frostbite was to rub snow on the frozen flesh!

CHAPTER 7
Alone in the Snow

Eight-year-old Walter Allen lived in the town of Groton in the Dakota Territory. On the morning of January 12, the temperature had climbed to twenty degrees, which must have felt like spring weather to Walter. That day, the four classrooms in the Groton School were full for the first time since Christmas because of the warmer weather. All of the children had small, rectangular chalkboard slates that they wrote on. On top of his school desk, Walter also had a prized possession—a beautiful glass perfume bottle filled with water. Walter would pour a drop of water  from the bottle onto his slate each time he needed to clean the slate and erase what he had written.

72

Around 10:30 a.m., a loud, roaring sound shook the building. The children rushed to the window. The formerly blue sky was filled with black clouds. As the outside temperature dropped, a snowstorm slammed against the schoolhouse, shaking its walls. Walter's teacher made a quick decision. The schoolchildren were told to dress quickly and return to their homes. But by the time the children from the four classrooms were ready to go, the blizzard had grown even stronger.

Some of the children were barely more than toddlers, and the teachers knew that they would never survive in the storm.

Just then, five horse-drawn sleds pulled up in front of the school. The men of Groton had moved quickly and placed large wooden platforms on top of the sleds so that they could load all of

the schoolchildren onto the platforms and carry them to safety. The snow was blowing so hard that Walter couldn't see more than a few inches in front of his face as he climbed up onto one of the sleds. When all of the children were safely on board, the sleds started moving slowly through the snowy streets.

Suddenly, Walter realized that he had forgotten his treasured water bottle. He jumped off the sled and struggled through the drifting snow to return to the deserted schoolhouse. It only took him a few minutes to grab his water bottle and run back outside. But by the time he had returned to the street, the sleds were nowhere to be seen.

Walter tried to walk in the direction of his home, but his eyes were covered in ice and started to freeze shut. He grew confused about which direction to go. The fierce wind knocked him down. Unable to stand, Walter curled up in the snow. As he stopped moving, the last sound Walter heard was the howling wind.

It wasn't until late in the afternoon, as the icy snow continued to fall, that the children were delivered safely to their homes. Walter's father, W. C. Allen, soon discovered that his son had not returned. He made a quick decision.

W. C. and his eighteen-year-old son, Will, would brave the storm and search for Walter. The men who had driven the sleds joined them.

As darkness fell on Groton and the snow
swirled around them, the search party returned to
the school. There was no sign of the missing boy.
Will lost his sense of direction in the storm and
wandered away from the other men. He struggled
to walk down the snowy street.

Will later remembered his thoughts as he searched for Walter. After they were all home safely, he planned to tease his younger brother and say, "Remember the time that damn fool of a boy ran off and hid in a blizzard and scared us all half to death? Just like Walter to pick the worst storm in history. The terrible blizzard of '88."

Eventually, Will bumped into a small pile of snow near the schoolhouse. Digging through the snow, he discovered Walter buried within it. The boy was unconscious but alive. Somehow Will managed to carry his brother through the blinding snow until they reached the Allen home. There, Walter drifted in and out of consciousness as his family slowly warmed the shivering boy. When Walter finally opened his eyes, he discovered that the water bottle in his pocket had frozen and burst during the blizzard. His precious water bottle had not made it through the storm, but Walter realized how lucky he was to have survived.

CHAPTER 8
Tragic Tales

Many children survived the storm, thanks to the heroic efforts of teachers, parents, and other brave individuals. On January 12, nearly every schoolteacher in the Great Plains faced a difficult decision. As the blizzard raged outside their schoolhouses, they had to decide quickly: Was it safer to have the children spend the night in their classrooms? Or should they journey out into the storm and try to lead their students to safe havens?

Farmers, business owners, and other adults also had to choose between two terrible options. Should they venture outside into the blinding storm and attempt to rescue people stranded in the snowdrifts? Or was it better to stay sheltered in their homes, waiting anxiously and hoping that family members would find their way to safety?

The Blizzard of 1888 had arrived without warning and struck at the worst possible time. Sadly, it claimed the lives of hundreds of children and adults.

The Westphalen sisters were two young girls who lived in Eastern Nebraska. They were thirteen-year-old Eda and eight-year-old Matilda, who were attending class on the afternoon of January 12 when the storm hit. Their teacher, Nellie Forsythe, decided to send all the children home, and the Westphalen sisters started making their way across a field near the school. The girls had the wind in their faces, and the blowing snow made it impossible for them to know which way to go. They walked in circles for a while and then finally sank to the ground as night fell. As they curled up together in a snowdrift, Eda wrapped her coat around her younger sister. It wasn't until the afternoon of Monday, January 16, that a search party located the girls. They had died the night of January 12. Matilda was still wrapped within the shawl of her older sister.

Another victim in Dakota Territory was a nun named Sister Ann Wilhelmina Kaufman. She worked in a laundry near the church. When she didn't return by noon during the blizzard, a search party tied a rope to the church and clung

85

to it. They searched the grounds near the church for hours during the blizzard. They found her crouching on the ground near a fence post, but the searchers were too late. Sister Kaufman had frozen to death.

One young hero of the storm was sixteen-year-old Omer Gibson. As the storm raged around his schoolhouse, he offered to escort his twelve-year-old niece, Amelia Shirk, to her home.

When they got lost in the snow, Omer wrapped a blanket around Amelia and told her to rest within a snowdrift. He walked away in search of help but soon collapsed and died. Amelia was found buried in the snow the next day. She had survived because of Omer's blanket.

A man named Robert Chambers was working on a farm in the Dakota Territory with his son Johnny and a Newfoundland dog when the blizzard hit. Robert and Johnny got lost in the storm while trying to move the cattle back to the barn. Robert wrapped Johnny in his jacket and vest and told the boy to huddle in a snowdrift. The father stood in the storm and shouted for help, but no one heard him over the howling winds. He then huddled close to his son and the dog, trying to keep Johnny warm. Sadly, that evening Robert froze to death. The next day, a search party heard the dog barking. Miraculously, they found Johnny still alive in the snowdrift.

Charles Birt was living in the southwestern part of the Dakota Territory near the present location of Ardmore, South Dakota. He later described what happened on January 12.

"It was very early in the morning of an unusually warm day that I went to the barn, about 120 yards from the house. I had been there only a short time when I heard a rushing, roaring sound in the west. It sounded like a freight train approaching. I hurried out to see the cause of the noise. I had reason to be uneasy when I got outside for the warm air was becoming icy and the sky was darkening as the storm struck. The wind came with almost tornado strength, and the snow was thick in the air. I started back to the house, fighting against the icy wind and thick snow, but was forced to get down on my hands and knees and crawl to make any progress. I thought I would never reach the house, but I did."

Great Plains residents like Charles Birt, Johnny Chambers, and Amelia Shirk were among the fortunate individuals who survived the blizzard. Hundreds of others were not so fortunate.

CHAPTER 9
After the Storm

The Children's Blizzard of 1888 lasted about twelve to eighteen hours and battered over a thousand miles of prairie land. After the storm, the temperatures stayed very cold, around twenty-five degrees below zero in many areas. There were huge piles of snow everywhere and an eerie silence.

The towns and cities in the region were at a standstill for days and sometimes weeks after the storm. Rescue parties made their way through the snowdrifts hoping to find missing family members and friends. Schools and businesses—including the local newspapers—were closed.

Telegraph lines were brought down by heavy snow, and trains were unable to move. The people living in the Great Plains were more isolated than ever.

The *Saint Paul Dispatch* newspaper in Minnesota printed one of the first stories about the blizzard in its afternoon edition on January 12. The next day stories on the storm appeared in

New York City and Chicago newspapers. After that, a flood of stories about the deadly blizzard started appearing in papers across the country. Because of the damaged telegraph lines and lack of train service throughout the Great Plains, most of those early stories lacked firsthand reports from people who lived in the areas hit by the storm.

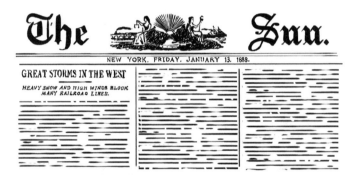

Clip from a New York newspaper in 1888

Some of the early stories were also inaccurate. One paper incorrectly reported that Walter Allen had died during the storm. Another, the *Omaha Daily Republican*, even *joked* about the blizzard, writing, "The local ice crop is assured."

The Railroad Comes to the Great Plains

During most of the first century of the nation's life, the area that would come to be known as the Great Plains was largely ignored. On maps it was sometimes called "the Great American Desert" or "Indian Territory." That changed in the mid-1800s, as railroads began to expand service to the Great Plains.

Taking advantage of millions of acres granted to them by the federal government, railroads laid down over 115,000 miles of new tracks in the prairie by 1880. Railroad officials chose locations and names for most of the region's new towns and cities. The railroad companies also printed up posters and brochures promising better lives on the Great Plains. Thousands of people from Europe and America's crowded East Coast cities boarded the new trains, hoping to find homes and farms they could call their own.

On January 13, the *Bismarck Weekly Tribune* called the blizzard "The Worst Storm in the Memory of the Oldest Inhabitant of the  Northwest." Two days later, *The Sun* newspaper in New York City had a front-page story listing many missing and dead victims of the storm. In just one paragraph alone, they listed eight victims: "At Minot, James Smith and two sons are missing. Two sons of William Driver of Raymond were frozen to death within a few feet of the farm barn. Charles Heath of the same place is missing. John Lay, a farm hand in Luverne, a veteran who served in the Fifth Minnesota Infantry, lost his way and was found dead. At Sioux Falls the body of a man was found last night frozen solid as also was the team of horses with him."

Newspapers tried to top each other to see who could come up with more dramatic headlines and stories. "THE RECORD OF THE DEAD" was a bold front-page headline in the *Chicago Tribune* on Saturday, January 21. Below that was listed "Thrilling Tales of Suffering from Exposure—Men and Women Perish on Their Own Premises—The Dire Distress of Passengers on a Blockaded Train—Babies Frozen in the Arms of Their Mothers."

In the days following the storm, newspaper estimates of the number of deaths varied widely, ranging from one or two hundred up to one thousand. Some of the newspapers with the higher estimates accused their competitors of deliberately lowering the number of deaths at the request of railroads and land companies that were hoping to promote the Great Plains as a desirable place to live.

In the end, the exact number of deaths was

never determined. Today, most historians and local state officials estimate that somewhere between 235 and 500 people died in the blizzard. Many of those victims were children. Those who choose the higher estimate of 500 believe that many deaths went unreported, especially in the more remote parts of the Great Plains. That higher number also includes people who may have died in the weeks or months after January 12, due to frostbite or other illnesses caused by the storm.

In addition to the loss of human life, thousands of farm animals also died, frozen within thick blocks of ice. Some of the animals were not discovered until the spring when the snows finally began to melt.

No one knows how many lives could have been saved if the Signal Corps had correctly predicted the blizzard and warned the people of the Great Plains in time. General Adolphus W. Greely was worried that the Signal Corps would be blamed for the many deaths and the massive amount of destruction. He issued a statement that said "the loss of life as given in the newspaper accounts has been doubtless exaggerated." Lieutenant Thomas Woodruff, who had sent the incomplete weather forecast on January 11, lost his job.

The problems of the Signal Corps didn't end with the blizzard in the Great Plains. Exactly two months later—on Monday, March 12, 1888—a dangerous blizzard hit New York City. Winds up to fifty miles per hour created twenty-five-foot-high snowdrifts. Streetcars were blown off their tracks and then buried in a tangled web of fallen electrical wires. The city was brought to a halt for days.

There had been no warning about the March blizzard because the Signal Corps offices in New York City had been closed from midnight Saturday until 5:00 p.m. on Sunday. The last forecast issued on Saturday night had predicted rain along with "colder fresh to brisk westerly winds, fair weather."

US Weather Bureau building, 1899

The Signal Corps was widely criticized for this mistake. After the New York blizzard, two changes were made. The Signal Corps weather stations now stayed open on Sundays. And in 1890 Congress moved the weather service—now called the US Weather Bureau—from the control of the army to that of the US Department of Agriculture. Greely was no longer in charge of weather forecasting.

The Children's Blizzard of 1888 was one of the worst disasters to ever hit the Midwest. It was created by a combination of three unfortunate events: dangerous weather, poor communication, and human error. It was just one day. But it was a single day that changed so much for so many people in this region.

Each year, on the anniversary date of January 12, people throughout the Midwest gather to remember the Children's Blizzard. They tell stories of the brave heroes who risked their lives to save others. And they honor the victims who died during the storm.

They gather together to make sure that this tragic event will never be forgotten.

Survivors of the Children's Blizzard gather in 1967 to remember the tragedy.

Timeline of the Children's Blizzard of 1888

1816 — Francis Ronalds creates the first working electric telegraph machine

1838 — Samuel Morse completes his code for sending telegrams

1860 — The United States Army Signal Corps is formed

1861 — The Dakota Territory is formed

1862 — US president Abraham Lincoln signs the Homestead Act

1870 — The US Army Signal Corps becomes responsible for weather forecasting

1880 — A blizzard known as the "Snow Winter" hits the upper Midwest and lasts for months

1886 — The "Winter of Blue Snow" blizzard begins; it will kill millions of cattle in the Great Plains

1887 — General Adolphus W. Greely is named head of the Army Signal Corps weather forecasting offices

1888 — The Children's Blizzard hits the Great Plains on January 12

— A deadly blizzard hits New York City and the surrounding areas on March 12

1890 — Responsibility for weather forecasting is transferred to the newly formed US Weather Bureau in the US Department of Agriculture

1967 — A mural depicting the Children's Blizzard of 1888 is installed in the Nebraska State Capitol building

Timeline of the World

1818 — Mary Shelley's *Frankenstein: The Modern Prometheus* is published

1840 — The first postage stamp is issued in England and features a profile of Queen Victoria

1861 — The US Civil War begins

1871 — The Great Chicago Fire burns down much of the city

1872 — Yellowstone becomes the first US National Park

1884 — Mark Twain's *The Adventures of Huckleberry Finn* is first published, in England

1885 — The Statue of Liberty is shipped from France to Bedloe's Island (now Liberty Island) in New York Harbor

1886 — Carl Benz patents one of the earliest automobiles, called the Motorwagen

— The first glass of Coca-Cola is sold

1889 — The Eiffel Tower opens in Paris, France

1900 — Construction of the New York City subway system begins

1901 — Britain's Queen Victoria dies at the age of eighty-one

— A working vacuum cleaner is invented by Hubert Cecil Booth

1903 — The Wright brothers take their first successful flight in a powered machine that is heavier than air

1967 — Batgirl makes her debut in *Detective Comics* no. 359

Bibliography

*Books for young readers

*Figley, Marty Rhodes. *The Schoolchildren's Blizzard*.
Minneapolis: Carolrhoda Books, Inc., 2004.

Idell, Albert E. *The Great Blizzard*. New York: Henry Holt and
Company, 1948.

*Kremer, Kevin. *Angel of the Prairie*. Osprey, FL: Kremer
Publishing, 2019.

Laskin, David. *The Children's Blizzard*. New York: HarperCollins
Publishers, 2004.

O'Gara, W. H. *In All Its Fury: A History of the Blizzard of
January 12, 1888*. Lincoln, NE: J & L Lee Books, 1988.

Sole, Bill. *Adams County: The First One Hundred Years*. Hastings,
NE: Huls Publishing Company, 1972.

*Tarshis, Lauren. *I Survived: The Children's Blizzard, 1888*.
New York: Scholastic Press, 2018.

*Yomtov, Nel. *The Children's Blizzard of 1888*. Minneapolis:
Lerner, 2017.